WHEA'
DI__ ___.

Lose the belly fat weight loss plan and wheat free recipe cookbook. Ideal diet for wheat, gluten and food allergy sufferers

By
Joshua Collins

Copyright

WHEAT FREE DIET: Lose the belly fat weight loss plan and wheat free recipe cookbook. Ideal diet for wheat, gluten and food allergy sufferers

By Joshua Collins

© Copyright 2013 Joshua Collins

This publication is designed to provide accurate and authoritative information in regard to the subject matter covered. It is sold the understanding that the publisher is not engaged in rendering legal, accounting, or other professional services. If legal advice or other expert assistance is required, the services of a competent professional person should be sought.

First Published, 2013

Printed in the United States of America

Table of Contents

Foreword 6

Introduction 8

What Is Wheat And Where Did It Come From? 10

5 Reasons Why You Should Consider A Wheat Free Diet 12

    Reason #1 – To Combat Chronic Tiredness 12

    Reason #2 – To Lose Weight 12

        Wheat Germ Agglutinin 13

        Gliadin 13

        Amylopectin A 13

    Reason #3 - The Cavemen Did Not Eat Wheat 14

    Reason #4 – To Avoid The Intake Of Preservatives And
Chemicals 14

    Reason #5 - To Fight Depression 14

The Healthy Advantages Of A Wheat-Free Diet 15

    You Will Feel And Look Healthier. 15

    You Will Save Money. 16

    Your Body Will Heal Faster 16

    Your Family Will Focus On Good Health 16

What On Earth Is The "Lose The Belly Fat Weight Loss Plan" 17

Medical Conditions That Benefit From A Wheat Free Diet 19

    Celiac Disease 19

    Diabetes (Or Pre-Diabetes) 20

    Gluten And Wheat Allergies 20

    Obesity 20

What Is A Wheat Allergy 21

Signs And Symptoms Of A Wheat Allergy 23

    Asthma 23

    Gastro Intestinal Symptoms 23

    Swelling Of The Mouth And Face 23

    Skin Rashes 23

    Headaches 24

Gluten-Free Versus Wheat Free 26

Are Celiac Disease And Wheat Allergies Different? 27

Foods And Condiments That Contain Wheat 28

How to Start and Implement a Wheat-Free Diet 30

Going Wheat-Free: Wheat Free Flours 32

Wheat Free Recipes That Are Healthy And Delicious 34

Delicious Breakfast Recipes 34

    Breakfast Burrito (Paleo Style) 35

    Sweet Green Smoothies 36

    Peanut Butter Flax Hot Cereal 37

    Baked Grapefruit 38

    Breakfast Casserole 39

Luscious Lunch Recipes 40

    Dreamy Macaroni & Cheese Style Spaghetti Squash 41

    Spicy Burgers 43

    Brown Rice Crust Quiche 45

    Goat Cheese And Roast Tomatoes Stuffed Portobello Mushrooms 47

    Healthy Gourmet Goulash 49

Delightful Dinner Recipes 50

    Honey-Lime Chicken Skewers Key West Style 51

    Mushroom Risotto 52

Taco Meatza 54

Wheat Free Bread And Pizza Crust Recipes 55

Wheat-Free Pizza Crust 56

Wheat Free Banana Bread 58

Wheat-free Garlic Bread 60

Snack Recipes 63

Creamy Yogurt Fresh Fruit Salad 64

Banana Ice Cream with a Twist 65

Dreamy Walnut Cake 66

Rosemary And Sea Salt Flax Crackers 67

Chocolate Mousse Shots 69

Dried Fruit Scones 70

Petite Raisin-White Chocolate Scones 72

Wheat-Free Recipes For Vegans 74

Patatas Bravas (Spicy Potatoes) 75

Teriyaki Eggplant Steaks 76

Mung Bean Stew 77

Baba Ganoush 78

Feedback From People Who Went On A Wheat Free Diet 79

Conclusion 80

Thank You For Buying This Book 81

Recommended Reads 82

Other Health Related Books By Joshua Collins 83

Medical Disclaimer 84

Foreword

By Dr. Rick Levine

Having been a health care provider for over 25 years I am always searching for information that I can be share with my patients which can have an impact on their health. I am a Chiropractor who utilizes nutrition as well as other holistic procedures extensively in my practice. Recently I came across an author named Joshua Collins whose work is informative, sometimes controversial, and always beneficial. He writes with passion and advocates the adoption of healthier lifestyles for anyone seeking to improve their current health situation.

Joshua Collins is what I consider a wellness expert who has extensive knowledge in the fields of nutrition, exercise and the mind-body connection. He shares his passion for helping others reach their health goals.

Joshua believes in viewing and treating the body as a whole. He understands that each person is unique based on their genetics, biochemistry, and psychological makeup. He understands that an individual's lifestyle choices in addition to environmental factors can have a huge impact on their health potential.

Joshua is a proponent of a holistic medical approach that focuses on identifying the root causes of disease rather than treating just the symptoms. He believes you must first understand the origins of chronic disease prior to the development of any meaningful treatment or preventive program.

He strives to help others improve their health by providing innovative, state of the art, health tips and information. He hopes to encourage you to make life-style changes that will both restore your health and ultimately help to prevent the onset of debilitating and life threatening chronic diseases.

For those who are interested in stabilizing and improving their health I recommend you read the books authored by Joshua Collins. At the very least, you will learn something new. I believe if you implement some of the lifestyle changes recommended in his books you will also improve your health. After all without our health we are not living up to our full potential.

Dr. Rick Levine a suburban Philadelphia Chiropractor and Nutritionist who has been educating and helping people restore their health for 25+ years.

Introduction

Millions of people all over the world are considered overweight or obese in this day and age. With the influx of fast-food restaurants and other preservative-filled foods, a lot of people settle for these nutrient depleted foods instead of seeking healthier alternatives. However, with the rising number of people who suffer from various diseases, many try to look for ways that they could improve their health and fitness. This is why various new diets, weight loss products, and exercise programs are introduced every day. Recently, there has been a trend towards removing wheat and wheat related products from one's diet. A famous expert, who published an extremely popular book, believes that wheat contributes to the development of heart disease, causes the joints to become inflamed and painful, and many more hard to pin down symptoms. Is this true, or is it a hoax?

This e-book discusses the many different theories concerning wheat, as well as the findings concerning a wheat-free diet. I will also include a section on some delicious wheat free recipes and do not worry if you are a vegan I have included some recipes that will work for you also. You will be surprised as to how beneficial the wheat-free diet can be when it comes to improving your health!

What Is Wheat And Where Did It Come From?

Wheat is actually a type of grass that is grown in many parts of the world and for tens of thousands of years has been thought to be nutritious. This cereal was originally grown in Ethiopian highlands, somewhere in the Near East, in the Levant region. Compared to any other commercially-raised food, this cereal grain is cultivated on more land and in more places around the world than any other type of food. Wheat is considered one of the primary sources of vegetable protein, containing more protein than soybeans and other major cereals such as rice, or corn.

In ancient history, wheat played a major role in the emergence of various city-states in what was called the Fertile Crescent, including the empires of Babylon and Assyria. Wheat was used as a staple in the diet of many civilizations and was made into flour. To date, wheat grain is still used to make flour for various foods such as breads, cakes, breakfast cereals, pastas, and as an additional ingredient for the fermentation of beer and other alcoholic beverages. There are even cases when wheat is used as a biofuel.

Wheat is also used as a forage crop for different types of livestock. The straw that is taken from the plant can also be used to make roofing thatch for construction purposes. Whole grain wheat can be milled so that the remaining product is the endosperm which is used for the production of white flour. The by-products of this milling process include germ and bran. Whole grain is a good source of protein, minerals, and vitamins, but the refined version is just mostly starch and devoid of the minerals and nutritional value of the whole grain variety.

5 Reasons Why You Should Consider A Wheat Free Diet

Although wheat is considered to be a nutritious food source, there have been studies conducted that have shown that wheat may actually contribute to many different health ailments and symptoms. Here are the some of the reasons why experts urge people to go on a wheat-free diet:

Reason #1 – To Combat Chronic Tiredness

If you suffer from the feelings of chronic tiredness and grogginess there may be a solution for you. Many alternative health practitioners encourage people to give up wheat because they believe that wheat causes imbalances in the body, especially in terms of minerals. Because of the lack of and in some cases the proper proportion of certain minerals in the body, people tend to feel tired and groggy.

Reason #2 – To Lose Weight

Wheat has been found to retain fluids in the body, which then results in weight gain. People who go wheat-free say that they have lost weight and were able to reduce the fluid retention and puffiness in their bodies. Wheat has been implicated as a cause of obesity and therefore may be considered an "Obesogen" which is simply a food that has the ability to make people gain weight easily.

Wheat contains the following ingredients which contribute to weight gain:

Wheat Germ Agglutinin

There have been experiments that have shown that wheat germ agglutinin has the capacity to bind to and block leptin which is a hormone that has the ability to make you feel satiated or full. When leptin is blocked by the wheat germ agglutinin it reduces the felling of satiety and amplifies your appetite causing you to eat more because you do not feel full. Leptin also plays a key role in regulating energy intake and energy expenditure and has a major effect on your metabolism.

Gliadin

Gliadin is the most abundant protein found in wheat. When gliadin is digested in the intestines it is broken down into polypeptides which are merely proteins broken down into amino acids. These amino acid chains bind to the opiate receptors found in the brain. However, these do not provide pain relief like opiates do, instead, they stimulate one's appetite and in certain situations can produce behavioral changes commonly found in ADHD, Manic Depression and other psychiatric disorders.

Amylopectin A

This is a complex carbohydrate that is found in wheat, and it is easily digested by the amylase enzyme found in one's saliva and secretions in the stomach. Because it is highly digestible it in theory, can cause a person's blood sugar spike upward quickly. This rather quick spike can have detrimental effects on blood sugar control and weight management.

Reason #3 - The Cavemen Did Not Eat Wheat

I know it sounds silly however one of the most probable theories why wheat intolerance is widespread is because the cavemen did not eat wheat. Wheat was only introduced about 10,000 years ago, along with the dawn of crop cultivation. The inclusion of wheat in man's diet is still considered a relatively new phenomenon compared to the diet of cavemen millions of years ago, consisting of fruits, berries, and nuts.

Reason #4 – To Avoid The Intake Of Preservatives And Chemicals

Unless you are 100% sure you are eating unaltered whole grain wheat in all probability it is processed and refined using preservatives, bleach, conditioners, and many other additives. There are times when the labels say that the wheat used is "whole" even when it has been processed. A lot of the fiber and nutrients have been stripped away in the refining process and is not the healthiest thing to be putting in your body on a daily basis.

Reason #5 - To Fight Depression

There have been studies conducted that indicate depression could actually be triggered by an intolerance to wheat. It has been said that the intestines are actually the main suspects and cures for many psychiatric disorders. Chemicals or toxins in the food that people eat, drugs, and other ingested materials could cause the intestines to become inflamed. When the intestines become inflamed they "leak" and then these unwanted elements are able to enter the bloodstream. This then can potentially lead to various disorders that are autoimmune in nature. The resultant improper nutrient absorption can affect brain chemistry. Alterations in brain chemistry can lead to depression and other psychiatric disorders.

These are just some of the many reasons why experts encourage people to go on a wheat-free diet. This may not be the perfect diet for everybody, but there are certainly some positive things that could happen to one's body when he or she goes wheat-free.

The Healthy Advantages Of A Wheat-Free Diet

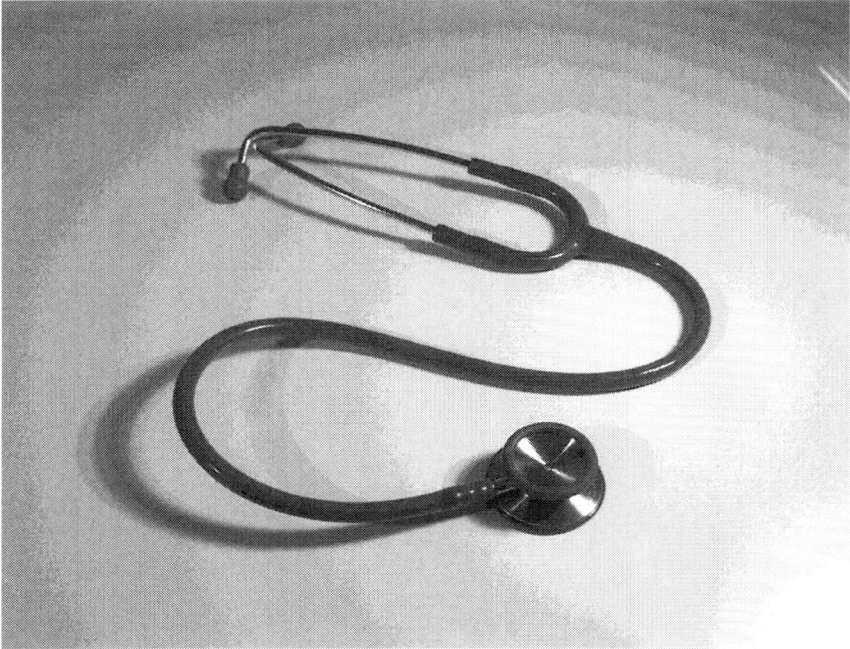

One of the most frequently questions I get asked is "What exactly are the advantages of going on a wheat-free diet?" If you check the internet, you can actually find a lot of articles that share the different benefits that you could experience from a changing to a wheat-free diet. Here are some of the advantages that you should know about if you are considering this type of eating program:

You Will Feel And Look Healthier.

When you choose to go wheat-free, you are actually opening yourself to the possibility of increasing the variety of whole foods into your diet. You do away with the processed foods of today, which are mostly made of over-processed ingredients like corn and wheat. By stocking up on lean meats, whole vegetables, grains, fruits, nuts, beans, and seeds, you are getting more vitamins and minerals. You will then see that you not only feel but also look healthier, and this can go a long way towards boosting your confidence and self-image, too!

You Will Save Money.

By choosing to go wheat-free, you will be looking for better food ingredients, including seasonal vegetables, which are usually cheaper to purchase from local markets. You also get more value when it comes to the nutrients you will get from these foods, compared to consuming processed meals and snacks.

Your Body Will Heal Faster

When you go wheat-free, you will see that many of the unpleasant symptoms brought about by various imbalances in your body start to vanish. Your body will enhance its ability to heal itself. Any cravings for pastas, breads, and other wheat-based products will disappear over time. Those who deal with chronic constipation, diarrhea, or bloating could feel a lot better when they go wheat-free.

Your Family Will Focus On Good Health

If you and your family decide to go wheat-free, you will all have fun trying to figure out what foods to eat, meal planning, what to cook, and a lot more. You can even let your children join in making healthier sweet snacks, and you may even help others who are skeptical and possibly misinformed about this diet!

As you see, these benefits do not only pertain to your own body, but with your relationship with others as well! These are the reasons why many people are already ditching wheat products and going for better and healthier alternatives.

What On Earth Is The "Lose The Belly Fat Weight Loss Plan?"

If you check the net, you will see a lot of discussions about diets which are designed to remove belly fat. However, I like to think in terms of an alternative way to eat as opposed to a diet. What is important to remember you are eating in a way to improve your health and one of the benefits of removing the wheat is you will experience weight loss.

The "Lose Belly Fat Weight Loss Plan" is all about taking out a substance that has been known to contribute to the development of various health problems, such as heart disease, foggy thinking, inflammation and pain of the joints, bloating, and a lot more. Weight loss is just one of the many benefits you will experience from removing wheat and its derivatives from your daily diet.

It is common knowledge in the nutritional field that wheat has contributed to the obesity problem that is an epidemic in many countries of the world. A lot of it lies in the genetic manipulation and the aggressive methods used to breed wheat, resulting to what has appropriately been called "Frankenwheat." One of the most frequent side effects to eating wheat is the uncontrollable cravings and urges to include more carbohydrates in one's diet.

As mentioned earlier in this e-book, grains were not originally part of the human diet. I personally am not on a crusade against wheat. What alarms me about wheat is its weight gaining properties and the many negative physiological effects it has on your body which have been spelled out in prior chapters. It simply makes sense that if you have a potential sensitivity to wheat or are diabetic or pre-diabetic that restricting carbohydrates in the wheat family makes a whole lot of sense.

 Remember that all carbohydrates you ingest get converted into glucose (or triglycerides if the cellular demand for fuel is low). Not only will your blood sugars improve but in addition you should see the reduction in your weight and triglyceride levels. Many individuals report that they were able to lose anywhere between 25-40 pounds in a six month time frame. Many also reported various benefits from going wheat-free, such as the reduction of irritable bowel syndrome symptoms, as well as the elimination of sorts of body pain. It is a simple concept to comprehend when people take wheat out of their diets, many of their health problems disappear. It isn't magic it's just normal physiology that occurs when you remove an irritant from your system.

Don't believe you can lose weight and improve your health? Just try eliminating wheat from your diet for 30 days. There have been reports that people felt younger and energetic when they follow the "Lose the belly fat weight loss plan. They also sleep better, are more flexible, have less joint pain and improve in many different ways. People who have skin problems also say that their skin issues have improved dramatically when removing wheat and its byproducts from your diet.

Medical Conditions That Benefit From A Wheat Free Diet

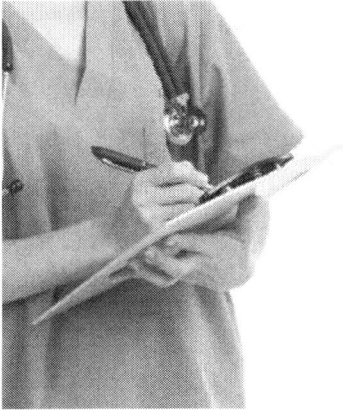

There are some medical conditions that have treatments that focus on the removal of wheat from the diets. Here is a list of the different conditions that can improve following a wheat-free diet:

Celiac Disease

Celiac disease is a genetic (inherited) disorder that makes the immune system of a person attack the small intestine when the person ingests gluten, a complex protein found in wheat, barley, and rye. The symptoms include the following: weight loss, abdominal pain, diarrhea, and delayed growth in children. Other non-digestive symptoms include anemia, skin rashes, bloating, and joint pain. Because of the many non-specific symptoms many of these individuals do not even know that they have celiac disease. Sometimes they suffer for years with these symptoms.

Diabetes (Or Pre-Diabetes)

People who have diabetes or those who are said to be approaching that disease are cautioned by their doctors to go on a low-sugar or low-carbohydrate diet. Wheat contains high levels of carbohydrates, which is converted to sugar by the body. By eliminating wheat and looking for better alternatives, diabetics will be able to manage their conditions better, as well as lose weight.

Gluten And Wheat Allergies

Of course, those who have wheat or gluten allergies should stay clear of wheat. Those who are hypersensitive to wheat should find other alternatives that are also healthier. That way, they can avoid suffering from allergies whenever they eat something that has wheat in it.

Obesity

Obesity is now a worldwide epidemic, and a lot of people have been saying that going wheat-free helps to lose weight. With proper exercise, people who are obese or overweight can lose weight, as well as improve their health. The cravings for more carbohydrates will also cease over time.

What Is A Wheat Allergy

I find that many people are confused about the difference between a wheat allergy and or intolerance and a gluten sensitivity which is found in Celiac disease. It is interesting to note that an allergy to wheat is one of the most common allergies found in children. To the dismay of many however, they are also found in adults.

People with a wheat allergy have an abnormal immune system response to at least one of the proteins that are present in wheat. By virtue of being an immune reaction the person with a wheat allergy develops a specific antibody to one or more of the proteins. The body's immune system, which normally is responsible for fighting infections, overreacts to the presence of these proteins in the body. When the person eats something that contains wheat, the immune system interprets these proteins as being dangerous and potentially harmful. Doing its job the immune system then responds by producing an allergic reaction in the body and this initiates the onset of symptoms which are associated with the wheat allergy.

The allergic reaction involves a substance known as IgE or immunoglobulin antibodies. The body's immune response is usually directed to at least one of the following proteins which are commonly found in wheat:
>   Albumin
>   Globulin
>   Gliadin
>   Glutenin (gluten)

Most allergic reactions to wheat involve albumin and globulin. An allergy to gliadin and gluten are less common and often associated with Celiac disease or other malabsorption diseases of the gastrointestinal system.

Below is a list of grains that should be avoided in an individual that has a wheat allergy:
>   Bran
>   Bread crumbs
>   Bulgur

Couscous
Durum, durum flour, and durum wheat
Einkorn
Farina
Farro (also known as emmer)
Kamut
Semolina
Sprouted wheat
Triticale
Wheat (bran, germ, gluten, grass, malt, starch)
Wheat berries
Wheat flour (all types, including all-purpose, cake,

Signs And Symptoms Of A Wheat Allergy

You may already be intolerant or allergic to wheat without knowing it! Here are the most common of signs and symptoms of wheat allergies:

Asthma

Asthma is known to be a common respiratory ailment that causes the airways to become constricted and inflamed. The following symptoms are usually associated with an asthma attack: chest tightness, coughing, shortness of breath, and wheezing. Though there are different causes of asthma, a wheat allergy could also be one of the initiating factors in an asthma attack.

Gastro Intestinal Symptoms

Whenever a person with wheat intolerance eats a food product that has wheat in it he or she may experience abdominal pain, vomiting, nausea, and bloating as well other digestive system symptoms

Swelling Of The Mouth And Face

Otherwise known as angioedema, this is a medical emergency that has to be treated right away or the person may go into anaphylactic shock.

Skin Rashes

A lot of food allergies, including wheat intolerance, can actually bring about the formation of skin rashes or hives. The skin could become dry, reddish, swollen, and itchy and very much look like eczema and psoriasis.

Headaches

The most common type of headache that is triggered by wheat intolerance is the sinus headache. Other common types are migraines and cluster headaches. Sinus headaches are those that include facial pain, and not necessarily felt in the head. Cluster headaches usually occur on just one side of the face or the head and usually produce pain in the back of or around the eye. Migraines are usually throbbing in nature and could be aggravated by light. Some people may even feel nauseous and vomit.

Wheat intolerance is a condition that also affects the immune system. This is due to the immune system's reaction to the breaking down of gluten, which may be perceived as being a "foreign" protein. This could then cause various inflammations in the body and disrupt various bodily processes.

Below are some additional signs and symptoms of a wheat allergy.

General:
tiredness, feelings of not being well, chronic fatigue, craving of foods

Immune conditions:
mouth ulcers, frequent infections like influenza and the common cold

Gastrointestinal:
constipation, flatulence, diarrhea, bloating, abdominal pain

Neurological:
memory loss, depression, behavioral difficulties, depression

Inflammatory conditions:
arthritis, allergies, colitis, stiff joints

Before you decide whether or not you are wheat intolerant or allergic, it is important to get yourself checked and properly diagnosed by a medical professional.

Gluten-Free Versus Wheat Free

When people say that it is best to go wheat-free, many equate it to going gluten-free. It is important for you to understand that wheat is not equal to gluten at all. A lot of foods that are labeled "wheat-free" actually still contain gluten, as gluten is found in other grains like rye, barley, and oats. Foods that are wheat-free can still have ingredients that are derived from these other grains and still have gluten in them.

The food labeling laws of the United States require that all manufacturers should indicate in the labels if they used wheat in their products, but not specify gluten. Wheat is considered one of the major allergens, so it is important that people are properly guided as to what ingredients are present in the food they eat.

Gluten-free foods and diets are centered more on those who suffer from celiac disease or those who have gluten intolerance or allergies. Wheat-free diets, however, focus on a wider range of people with a broader range of symptoms.

Are Celiac Disease And Wheat Allergies Different?

Celiac disease and a wheat allergy are often confused but in reality they are quite different. Celiac disease is caused by a localized inflammatory reaction in the small intestines caused by gluten. As a result of this inflammatory reaction the cells lining the small intestine become unable to properly absorb nutrients. This malabsorption leads to all of the symptoms associated with Celiac disease.

Wheat allergies on the other hand produce a more generalized immune response and produce more generalized symptoms and are not limited to the digestive tract. Some of the most common symptoms are breathing difficulties, nausea, hives, bloated stomach and an inability to focus. With some people the consumption of wheat and wheat products may result in a systemic reaction called "anaphylaxis" which can be life threatening.

Individuals with a wheat allergy can usually eat other grains however individuals who suffer from Celiac disease cannot eat any food containing gluten. Gluten can be found in other grains such as barley and rye. Some people also are sensitive to oats and it too is oftentimes added to the list of foods one cannot eat if they suffer from Celiac disease.

Foods And Condiments That Contain Wheat

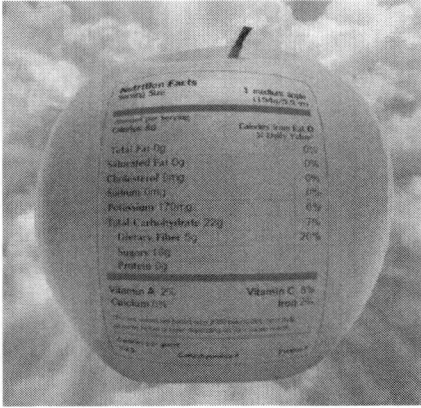

If you are not fond of label-reading, you may not know that many of the foods you buy actually have wheat in them. Here is short list of the foods and condiments that have wheat as an ingredient but make sure to check all labels:

Beer/Ale
Brown rice syrup
Condiments that are made using grain distilled vinegar
Some canned tuna, alcohol-based extracts, dips, cheese spreads,
Emulsifiers
Dextrin
Gluten stabilizers
Food that is fried in restaurants
Oat gum
Packaged pudding
Graham
Herbal teas that are made using malted barley
Canned black-eyed peas
Spaghetti or Marinara sauce
Imitation bacon
Cooked pork bacon
Processed and frozen meats
Pastas
Breads

Crackers (salting)
Flour tortilla
Blue cheese
Low-fat cottage cheese
Non-dairy creamers
Egg substitutes
Non-fat sour cream
Soy milk
Dry cocoa mixes
Bean paste
Mayonnaise
Tofu
Curry powder
Soy sauce
Ketchup
Mustard
Walnut extract
Worcestershire sauce
Yeast extract or instant dry yeast
Allspice
Pickles
Relish
Ground ginger
Cumin
Cayenne pepper
Nutmeg
Seven spice seasoning
Commercial candies, colorings, corn syrups, preservatives, and flavorings

How to Start and Implement a Wheat-Free Diet

According to some experts, as we have discussed in prior chapters, wheat is connected to many diseases and chronic symptoms that are quite common in our society today. As a result of the abundance of information available about the potential negative health consequences of eating wheat there are many people who are already looking into removing wheat from their daily diets in an effort to live healthier lives.

One of the most difficult stumbling blocks for many is where to start and how to implement such a change in the way they eat. The best way to start this new way of eating is to always read labels of food you purchase first and foremost. Next you need to identify and get rid of foods at home that have wheat as an ingredient. Lastly you should avoid recipes and foods that contain the wheat. It also helps to write down a list of the foods and ingredients to avoid and attach it to the refrigerator, so that you can remind yourself of products that you should avoid.

In starting a wheat-free diet, it is ultra-important to read labels on all food products you purchase. There are a lot of food items you probably consume that contain wheat (see chapter on foods and condiments that contain wheat) as well as its derivatives. Foods like pastas and breads, unless labeled as wheat or gluten free, usually are made from wheat so they should be taken off the shopping list if you are on a wheat-free diet. There are also some seasonings that may contain wheat as an ingredient.

When shopping in the market I tend to shop in the perimeter of the store. That is usually where the fresh fruits and vegetables and fresh meats are located and these fresh foods are the backbone of any healthy eating program. Nuts are also highly recommended due to the fact they are a good protein source and contain natural oils which are beneficial to your health.

Recipes that call for flour, breadcrumbs, and breaded or flour coatings, do not have to be avoided as there are many alternatives available that are both safe and delicious. In the next section we will be discussing these alternatives so you can easily start you wheat free eating plan.

As stated above starting and implementing a wheat-free diet can be done and it actually gets easier as you get used to the new way of eating. Like anything in life change can sometimes be a little scary but if you make a commitment to improving your health you will succeed.

Going Wheat-Free: Wheat Free Flours

Because of the genetic manipulation performed on wheat in an effort to create a crop that has higher yields, the nutrients that were found in prehistoric wheat have been vastly depleted in the modern version of the crop. This is why many experts in the field of nutritional science shun away from wheat in their diets in favor of foods that are wheat-free and have not been stripped of their nutritional value.

Since wheat-free dieters have to substitute wheat with other more viable and healthier options, it is important to know which flours are free of wheat agglutinin. There are many people who worry needlessly that they may not be able to find substitutes for the regular wheat flour that they use in their cooking. Rest assured that there are actually a lot of alternatives that are both healthy and delicious! There are a lot of grains, starches, thickeners, and flours that are wheat-free and are listed below. These alternatives are plentiful and are easily substituted for wheat flour in your favorite recipes.

Here is a list of wheat free flours that are safe to use in all your favorite recipes:

- **Buckwheat flour**
Though the name "buckwheat" has the word "wheat" in it, it is an herbal plant. The fruit that this plant produces is somewhat similar to the seed of a sunflower. It is this fruit that is ground to create the flour like substance.

- **Flax seed meal**
This flour alternative is made from ground flax seeds. Flax Seed meal is known to be very high in omega fatty acids and protein.

- **Rice flour** (white, sweet/glutinous rice, and brown)

- **Quinoa flour**

- **Sorghum flour**

- **Millet flour**

- **Amaranth flour**

- **Coconut flour** – This is my personal favorite
 This flour is created by grinding coconut meat. This flour is nearly carbohydrate free and is an added bonus for dieters.

- **Nut flours** (almond, pecan, cashew, chestnuts)

- **Teff flour**

- **Soy, chick pea, garbanzo, and bean flours**

- **Potato flour**

- **Yam and sweet potato flour**

My recommendation is to try all of the above flour alternatives and see which ones you like the most. Once you have identified your favorites they you can substitute those flours into recipes that call for wheat flour. However, cooking times may vary, so it may take some experimentation on the part of the user to determine how long they have to cook the food.

As you can see from the list above there are a many wheat and gluten free substitutes for wheat flour in the market. You will be surprised how different you can feel once you get on a wheat-free diet.

Wheat Free Recipes That Are Healthy And Delicious

In this part of the e-book, I would like to share some great recipes for you and your family. As mentioned earlier, going wheat-free does not have to be a sad affair at all! Feel free to check out the recipes below and choose the ones that you think are a good fit for you.

Delicious Breakfast Recipes

You can really get creative and make some incredible dishes for breakfast. Why not start off your day with these healthy dishes. Here are some of my favorites!

Breakfast Burrito (Paleo Style)

Ingredients:

Sliced ham (medium thick slices)
2 eggs or egg whites
A quarter cup of chopped vegetables (bell pepper, tomato, spinach, and a lot more)
Optional: guacamole, cilantro, salsa, lettuce (any kind)

Preparation:

- Sauté the chopped vegetables in a little bit of olive or coconut oil over medium high heat.

- Whisk the eggs in a small bowl and pour over the sautéed vegetables.

- Scramble the mix until it is fully cooked through. Take it out of the pan.

- Put the egg and vegetable mix on a medium thick slice of ham and roll it up.

- Place it back on the skillet and grill until the ham turns slightly brown.

-You have the option to wrap the ham and egg with lettuce. You can then serve it with guacamole, salsa, and fresh cilantro.

Sweet Green Smoothies

This is an excellent liquid meal as it has a good mix of carbohydrates, fat, and protein.

Ingredients:

-2 large kale leaves
-Half cup raw cashews (It is best that you soak it about 2-4 hours ahead of time)
1 apple
1 banana
1 large carrot
1-2 cups of water
10 drops liquid stevia
2 handfuls of ice

Preparation:

-Drain and rinse soaked cashews and put in the blender.

-Chop vegetables and fruits lightly and add to the blender.

-Add 1 cup of water and blend everything until the mixture is almost smooth.

-Add ice and continue to blend until the mixture is very smooth and creamy.

-Additional water is optional, depending on the consistency that you want.

-Serve immediately.

Peanut Butter Flax Hot Cereal

Ingredients:

-4 tablespoons flax meal
-2 tablespoons peanut butter
-¼ teaspoon cinnamon
-½ cup boiling water

Preparation:

-Add boiling water over the flax meal and mix.

-Combine the cinnamon and peanut butter. Make sure it's incorporated by mixing well.

-Allow it to thicken for about a minute or two.

Baked Grapefruit

A unique way to eat a grapefruit!

Ingredients:

-2 grapefruits

-Approximately 4 tablespoons of honey (You can also use other sweeteners of your choice, such as Maple syrup. The amount to be used actually depends on your taste, as well as the size of the grapefruits you will be using.)

-A teaspoon of cinnamon (You can use more or less, depending on grapefruit's size.)

Preparation:

-Preheat the oven to 375 degrees Fahrenheit. Wash and carefully cut the grapefruit into 2 parts (halves).

-To loosen the fleshy part, cut along the sections and the skin.
-Drizzle about one tablespoon of honey on the top of each half. Make sure that you also put honey at the center, too. You can then sprinkle cinnamon on top.

-Pop the halves into the oven and bake for about 15 minutes. Once the edges look like they are starting to brown, they are done. Take out the flesh using a spoon and enjoy your baked grapefruit!

Breakfast Casserole

Ingredients:

-Sweet potato, diced (1 if using a large one, 2 if using medium ones)
-1 pound breakfast sausage
-1 diced green onion
-2-3 cups of chopped fresh baby spinach
-10 to 12 eggs (large)
-Sea salt plus fresh ground pepper

Preparation:

-Preheat the oven to 375 degrees. Grease a glass baking dish (9"x13") with coconut oil.

-Using medium-high heat, heat your skillet. Take the sausage out of its casing and cook until it has browned.

-Remove the cooked sausage and set aside. Set aside the remaining oil from the sausage.

-Add the sweet potatoes to the skillet with the leftover grease, and leave them to cook until they are tender. Remember to stir occasionally, approximately every 10 to 15 minutes.

-Once done, remove the sweet potatoes and place them in a bowl. Toss in the spinach, sausage, and green onion. Add salt and pepper. Mix them well.

-Place the mix into the glass dish. Be sure to spread it evenly.

-In another big bowl, whisk the eggs. Pour the egg mixture over the vegetable and sausage mixture. Bake it in the oven for about 25 to 30 minutes, until the egg has set.

-Let the casserole cool before serving. Cut into squares and dig in!

Luscious Lunch Recipes

There are a lot of possibilities for a wheat-free lunch. I have included some of my favorite mouthwatering recipes for you. You can also get creative and add additional ingredients to add a personal touch to the recipes. Bon Appetite!

Dreamy Macaroni & Cheese Style Spaghetti Squash

This is a creamy and cheesy lunch for one.

Ingredients:

-1 ½ cups cooked spaghetti squash
-½ tablespoon of wheat free flour (coconut, almond, rice, flax seed meal to name a few)
-¼ cup 1% milk
-1 tablespoon frozen peas
-1 slice green pepper (finely diced)
-¼ cup shredded cheese (Tex-Mex blend)
-1 tablespoon shredded Parmesan cheese
-1 finely diced green onion
-Salt and pepper

Preparation:

-Preheat oven to 350 degrees. Using cooking spray, spray the bottom and the sides of a casserole dish and set aside.

-In a saucepan (small), whisk flour, salt, and pepper together, over medium heat.

-Add in milk slowly until the mixture becomes smooth. Stir and cook until mixture thickens.

-Remove from heat and add the shredded Tex-Mex blend cheese. Stir until smooth and fully melted.

-Pour cheese sauce over the spaghetti squash and combine well in a bowl.

-Spread the mixture onto the casserole dish.

-Sprinkle the top with the onion, peas, green pepper, and Parmesan cheese.

-Bake at 350 degrees for 20 minutes or until the cheese has melted and the spaghetti squash has been heated all the way through.

Spicy Burgers

This is a great treat for those who love burgers and spices.

Ingredients:

-16 ounces of extra lean ground beef, lamb, or bison
-1.7 ounces of breadcrumbs (wheat or gluten-free)
-1 large onion, finely chopped
-2 teaspoons olive oil
-1 tablespoon garam masala (yes it is a real spice)
-1 teaspoon ground cinnamon
-1.7 ounces of chopped almonds
-1 large carrot, peeled and grated
-1 lemon, grated (zest)
-1 large egg, beaten
-Olive oil for frying
-Freshly ground black pepper

Preparation:

-In a large pan, heat the olive oil and add the onion until it becomes soft and golden.

-Add the cinnamon and garam masala and cook for about a minute. Remove the pan from heat and tip the contents into a big bowl. Set the pan aside.

-Add the ground lamb or beef, almonds, carrot, breadcrumbs, and the lemon zest to the bowl that contains the onion mixture. Combine the ingredients well. Season with black pepper and add the beaten egg. Mix well again.

-Divide the mixture into 8 parts, and shape each part into a burger.

-Heat a small amount of olive oil in the pan used previously. Place the burgers on the pan and be sure to sear them quickly on each side.

-Remove them from the pan and place on a baking tray (non-stick).

-Bake the burgers for about 15 minutes or so, until they are cooked through.

-You can serve the burgers with a wheat-free roll, with mango chutney and lettuce.

Brown Rice Crust Quiche

If you love quiche you will love this wheat free variety. It is delicious and incorporates leftover brown rice.

Ingredients:

For the brown rice crust

-1 ½ cups of cooked brown rice
-1 egg

For the filling

-1 cup milk (you can also use a milk substitute such as almond milk)
-4 eggs
-2 cups of filling (you can choose from different types to be presented below)
-¼ teaspoon of salt
-¼ teaspoon of pepper

Preparation:

-Preheat the oven to 350 degrees. Mix the rice with the egg (1 egg).

-Place the mixture on a 9" tart or pie pan. Be sure to spread it evenly, including the sides of the pan. You can either grease the pan beforehand or not.

-Bake the crust for about 10-15 minutes or until it becomes golden in color. Set aside.

-Whisk the ingredients for the filling together. Pour the mixture onto the crust.

-Bake it at 350 degrees for about 45 minutes, or until you see a toothpick comes out clean after you insert it at the center.

-Let the quiche cool for about 10 minutes before you slice it up and serve.

You can choose to substitute the whole egg with egg whites. The different suggestions for fillings include the following:

Vegetarians: Chopped onions, spinach, tomatoes, and bell peppers

Meat Lovers: Pepperoni, bacon, turkey, salami, ham

Mediterranean: Roasted red peppers, kalamata olives, capers, artichoke hearts

Hawaiian: Onions, pineapple, Canadian bacon

Leftovers: Check your fridge for any leftovers and pop them in your quiche.

Goat Cheese And Roast Tomatoes Stuffed Portobello Mushrooms

This meaty mushroom dish will simply take your breath away.

Ingredients:

-4 Portobello mushrooms, approximately about 4 inches across
-3 tbsp. olive oil
-2 tsp. shallot, finely chopped (This is optional.)
-1 tbsp. lemon juice
-1 garlic clove (large), finely chopped
-4 ounces goat cheese (plain)
-1 tbsp. fresh chopped chives
-1 tbsp. fresh chopped parsley
-Oven roasted tomatoes
-Salt and pepper

Preparation:

-Clean the Portobello mushrooms by wiping the outer part of the caps gently,using a damp paper towel, or brush off any dirt using a soft brush.

-Take out the stems by pushing them from one side to another until they snap off. Using a teaspoon, scrape the gills of the mushroom until the part under the mushroom is clean.

-Place the mushrooms on rimmed baking sheet with a foil lining.

-Mix lemon juice, garlic, shallot, and olive oil together. Brush the mushroom caps inside and out with the mixture. You should then sprinkle each cap with pepper and salt.

-Preheat the broiler. Be sure to place the oven rack on the level just below the top level.

-Broil the mushrooms for about 3 to 5 minutes until the edges start to brown and the mushrooms become hot. Notice that they will become juicy and release moisture.

-Remove mushrooms from the oven.

-Preheat oven to 375 degrees Fahrenheit. Meanwhile, fill the mushroom caps with roasted tomatoes and dot them with goat cheese. Sprinkle them with fresh herbs.

-Bake the mushrooms for 12 minutes or until the cheese has softened. You can brush the edges of the caps with extra olive oil to make them shinier and serve.

Healthy Gourmet Goulash

Ingredients:

-1 cup elbow noodles (gluten-free: rice noodles are my favorite)
-1 pound ground beef (For a vegan version, you can omit this by adding extra
   vegetables.)
-2 cups diced tomatoes (some use the canned variety)
-2 carrots, chopped
-2 zucchinis, chopped
-1 onion (large), chopped
-2 15-ounce cans of your favorite beans (You can use kidney and garbanzo beans)
-1 garlic clove, minced
-1 teaspoon each of paprika and oregano
-Salt and pepper

Preparation:

-Cook ground beef and the chopped onion in a skillet over medium heat. While doing this, you can cook the elbow noodles according to the instructions on the package.

-Mix the cooked noodles, beans, chopped vegetables, and spices in a big saucepan. You can then add the onion and beef mixture.

-Let everything simmer on medium-low heat for about 20 minutes or until the carrots become soft.

-Enjoy your lunch!

Delightful Dinner Recipes

There are also a lot of choices for a healthy and nutritious dinner. Here are some of my favorites. Enjoy!

Honey-Lime Chicken Skewers Key West Style

These are great for those who love kebabs. Chicken lovers are also in for a treat with this amazing recipe.

Ingredients:

-1 pound skinless and boneless chicken breasts
-2 tablespoons cilantro
-3 tablespoons soy sauce (check to make sure it is wheat-free)
-1 tablespoon coconut oil
-2 tablespoons honey
-Juice from one lime
-1 to 2 teaspoons Siracha
-2 minced garlic cloves
-Red pepper flakes, to taste

Preparation:

-In a small bowl, mix all ingredients except for the chicken. Be sure to combine everything thoroughly.

-Pour the marinade over the chicken breasts and turn to coat them fully. Cover and allow the marinade to soak in for at least an hour.

-Grill the chicken on medium high heat for 6-8 minutes per side. You will know when it's done when the juices run clear.

Note: If you are going to use bamboo skewers, be sure to soak the sticks for at least 5 minutes. Cut the chicken breasts into large chunks and skewer. Allow them to marinate for at least an hour.

Mushroom Risotto

This is an Italian-style risotto, which means that the result will be soft and creamy once fully cooked. This can be a main course or a side dish. This is perfect for cold nights.

Ingredients:

-7 ounces risotto rice (Arborio)
-1 onion, chopped
-1 green pepper, chopped
-1 red pepper, chopped
-2 tablespoons olive oil
-7 ounces grams assorted mushrooms, sliced
-750 ml wheat-free or gluten-free vegetable stock
-2 teaspoons dried oregano
-1.7 ounces of parmesan cheese, grated (for vegan version, omit this or use dairy-free parmesan)
-Additional boiling water
-Freshly ground black pepper

Preparation:

-In a heavy-bottomed pan, put 2 tablespoon olive oil or coconut oil and add the rice. Gently heat the rice for about 2-3 minutes, until the rice looks translucent.

-Add the onion, mushrooms, and peppers, and cook for another 5 minutes. Be careful not to brown the rice.

-Add vegetable stock and bring to a boil. Reduce the heat and simmer the rice for about 25 minutes. Add boiling water as necessary, to make sure that the mixture does not dry out.

-When cooking is done, the risotto should be moist, soft, and creamy, not dry. It is better to leave the risotto slightly wetter than come up with a dry one.

-Add the oregano and black pepper. Mix well.

-Serve with grated parmesan on top, or for a vegan version, with dairy-free parmesan.

Taco Meatza

Here is a great recipe for the taco lovers out there.

Ingredients:

-2 pounds ground beef
-1 teaspoon salt
-1 package Taco seasoning (or you can make your own out of 1 teaspoon garlic powder, 2 teaspoons chili powder, ½ teaspoon paprika, and 1 teaspoon ground cumin)
-1 egg
-½ chopped onion for the toppings
-1 cup cooked rice (or tortilla chips that have been crushed)
-1 cup salsa
-1 cup black beans
-1 cup vegetables, chopped (You can use any combination.)
-Optional toppings: lettuce, tomatoes, black olives, guacamole, and cheese

Preparation:

-Preheat oven to 450 degrees. Combine all of the ingredients for the crust and spread it on a baking sheet.

-Bake it for 10 minutes. You will see that it will get smaller. Drain the excess beef fat.

-Put salsa on the crust, rice or tortilla chips, black beans, and the chopped vegetables. Broil it until it becomes golden brown and serve.

Wheat Free Bread And Pizza Crust Recipes

I am aware that many people who embark on a healthier way to eat via a wheat free diet oftentimes have difficulty sticking to the plan. Oftentimes this is due to the fact that they miss and crave bread and its related products. I have put together some fantastic wheat free bread alternatives that you will find to be both satisfying and delicious and will overcome your stumbling block to giving up breads as you switch to a much healthier wheat free diet. Bon Appetite!

Wheat-Free Pizza Crust

This is ideal for pizza lovers wishing for a wheat-free crust. Just toss your favorite ingredients on it and you are all set!

Ingredients:

1 ½ cups of brown rice flour
2 tablespoons non-fat milk powder (dry) or buttermilk powder
1 teaspoon of baking powder
1-tablespoon honey or sugar
¾ teaspoon of salt
1 teaspoon of xanthan gum
1-cup warm water
1 ½ teaspoons of instant yeast
2 tablespoons of olive oil for the dough
2 tablespoons of olive oil for the pan

Preparation:

- Preheat the oven to 425 degrees Fahrenheit.

- Put all of the dry ingredients, except for the yeast, in a large mixing bowl. The stand mixer's bowl is perfect for this. Mix everything until thoroughly incorporated.

- In a small bowl, add in the olive oil, warm water, yeast, and about half of the dry mixture. Stir until everything is combined. If there are still some lumps, that's okay.

- Leave the mixture for about 30 minutes. You will see that the mixture becomes bubbly and will start to have a yeasty smell.

- Add the previous mixture to the remaining dry ingredients. Beat everything on medium-high speed for about 4 minutes. The resulting mixture will be sticky and thick. It is best to use a stand or electric hand mixer to make sure everything is well incorporated. Hand mixing does not seem to be good enough.

- Let the dough rest while covered for about 30 minutes or so.

- Drizzle the 2 tablespoons of olive oil onto a baking sheet or a 12" diameter pizza pan. Take out the dough from the bowl and on the oil puddle.

- With wet fingers, start working the dough outwards starting at the center.   Press it into a 12- to 14-inch circle.

- Let the dough rest again for 15 minutes, this time without a cover.

- Bake it for about 8-10 minutes or until everything is set. You will know it when the surface starts looking opaque instead of shiny.

- Remove this from the oven and then top it with anything that you want. Return everything to the oven for about 10-15 minutes, or depending on the toppings that you have chosen.

- Serve warm.

Nutritional Facts:

Serving size: 1/8 (one slice) of the recipe
Per serving:
Calories: 152
Calories from fat: 60
Total Fat: 5 grams
Sodium: 284 milligrams
Carbohydrate: 25 grams
Dietary Fiber: 1 gram
Sugar: 3 grams
Protein: 2 grams

Wheat Free Banana Bread

This is a great alternative to the yummy banana bread that Mom used to make. Although this recipe is not traditional bread I included it here because some people enjoy banana bread with a meal. It would go perfect with a salad and it is a great recipe to make if you have leftover bananas at home.

Ingredients:

2 cups of corn flour
1 teaspoon of baking soda
4 eggs
¼ teaspoon of salt
2 cups of ripe bananas, mashed (around 4-5 medium bananas)
1 cup of sugar
1/3 cup of sunflower oil
½ cup of unsweetened applesauce
1 teaspoon of vanilla extract
½ cup chopped pecans

Preparation:

- Preheat the oven to 350° Fahrenheit.

- In a big bowl, mix the salt, corn flour, and baking soda. Make sure that everything is mixed well.

- In a small bowl, whisk the sugar, eggs, oil, bananas, and vanilla. Make sure that everything is well incorporated.

- Add the wet mixture to the dry ingredients and stir until the dry ingredients are moistened.

- Coat the surfaces of 2 8x4-inch loaf pans with cooking spray. Sprinkle the bottom with the chopped pecans. Pour the mixture into the two loaf pans.

- Bake the bread for about 45-55 minutes. You can check if it's already cooked through the toothpick test (insert a toothpick near the center of the bread and it should come out clean).

- Cool the bread for about 10 minutes or so before you take them out from the loaf pans and onto wire racks.

- This bread is perfect together with tea or coffee. For those who wish to have a cool treat for warm days, this bread also works well when left in the refrigerator to cool.

Nutritional Facts:

A slice of banana bread is equal to:
Calories: 140
Fat: 6 grams
Saturated Fat: 1 gram
Cholesterol: 35 milligrams
Sodium: 89 milligrams
Carbohydrate: 21 grams
Protein: 3 grams

Wheat-free Garlic Bread

For garlic bread lovers out there, this wheat-free version is a delight. This recipe needs to be kneaded, just like the traditional way of making bread. Enjoy this wheat free Italian favorite.

Ingredients:

Wet ingredients
- 1/3 cup of whole psyllium husks
- 1/3 cup of ground chia seeds
- 2 ½ cups of warm water (about 105-110°F)
- 1 teaspoon honey
- 2 tablespoons maple syrup
- 2 ¼ teaspoons of active dry yeast
- 2 tablespoons of extra virgin olive oil (plus extra for topping)

Dry ingredients
    1 cup sorghum flour
    ½ cup sweet rice flour
    1 cup teff flour
    ½ cup almond meal
    1 ½ teaspoons of sea salt

Topping
    Freshly chopped garlic
    Poppy seeds
    Sesame seeds

Steps:

- When you buy whole chia seeds, use a coffee grinder to grind them. Store the   ground chia seeds in a glass jar and pop it in the refrigerator only until a week.

- Preheat the oven to 400° Fahrenheit.

- Put the warm water in a bowl. Combine a teaspoon of honey and the yeast and whisk them together. Leave the mixture for about 5-10 minutes to let the yeast activate. The mixture should become bubbly or foamy. If this does not happen, discard the mixture and start over.

- While the yeast is being activated, you can start mixing the dry ingredients in a big bowl.

- When the yeast is activated, add in the maple syrup, olive oil, psyllium husks, and ground chia seeds into the mixture. Leave the mixture for about 2-3 minutes (this is important, so watch the time) to let the psyllium and the chia seeds release a gelatin-like substance. Whisk these together.

- Pour all the wet ingredients into the bowl with the dry ingredients. Mix everything together using a wooden spoon until the mixture becomes thick. On a floured wooden board, knead the dough to mix in the flour. Add the freshly chopped garlic as you knead. Add more of the sorghum and teff flours, a little at a time. Continue adding until the dough holds but is still a bit sticky to the touch.

- Make a ball with the dough and put it back into the big bowl. Cover it with a damp towel. Place the bowl in a warm spot so that the dough rises. Some place the bowl on a pot that has warm water. Let it rise until the dough is doubled in size.

- When the dough has risen, put a pizza stone inside the oven. Put a pan of water on the bottom rack, just beneath the pizza stone. You can use an 8x8-inch glass pan filled with water (about ¾ of the way).

- Punch the dough down and lay it out onto a wooden board that has been lightly floured. Knead it for about a minute and then form it into a ball. Place the dough on a square piece of parchment paper. Using a sharp knife, create a shallow pattern on top (a tic-tac-toe pattern). Drizzle the top with olive oil, and then sprinkle with sesame and poppy seeds. Let the dough rise for 30 minutes more in a warm place.

- Carefully lift the parchment paper with the dough, and place it on the stone inside the oven. Bake the bread for 40 minutes.

- Remove the bread from the oven once cooked, and let it cool for about 30-60 minutes before cutting it. The bread is still a bit gummy in texture when hot and fresh out of the oven.

Nutrition facts:

1 slice (if the loaf is divided into 15 slices) is equal to:
Calories: 161
Fat: 6 grams
Sodium: 200 milligrams
Carbohydrates: 24 grams
Fiber: 5.5 grams
Protein: 4 grams
Calcium: 5%
Iron: 6%
Selenium: 6%

Snack Recipes

There are truly a lot of options for wheat-free snacks! You can even concoct your own snacks at home, using ingredients that you have on hand. Here are some great snack recipes for you.

Creamy Yogurt Fresh Fruit Salad

Ingredients:

-2 cups strawberries, sliced
-2 bananas, sliced
-2 fresh peaches, sliced
-2 cups grapes
-1 8-ounce container of vanilla or plain yogurt
-1 teaspoon sugar
-2 teaspoons lemon juice
-½ teaspoon vanilla extract
-Lime juice

Preparation:

-Mix all the fruit together in a big bowl

-Mix in about 3 tablespoons of lime juice to prevent the fruits from going brown. This also helps to boost the flavor.

-Mix yogurt, sugar, lemon juice, and vanilla in a small bowl.

-You have the option to either serve the yogurt mix as a dip for the fruits, or mix it right in with the fruit to create a salad.
-Serve right away

Banana Ice Cream with a Twist

Ingredients:

-4 bananas that are slightly overripe, sliced and frozen
-2 tablespoons creamy peanut butter
-2 teaspoons cocoa powder
-Optional: milk

Preparation:

-Place frozen banana slices in a food processor and pulse.

-You can add milk to help the bananas to blend faster.

-When the bananas start to look like whipped ice cream, you can add in the peanut butter and cocoa powder.

-For a soft-serve ice cream texture, serve it right away. For a firmer texture, you can pop it in the freezer first.

Dreamy Walnut Cake

Ingredients:

-½ cup black walnuts
-1 ½ cups English walnuts
-1 cup sugar (divided into portions of two ¼ cups and ½ cup)
-2 ounces butter
-¼ teaspoon salt
-4 egg whites
-4 egg yolks

Preparation:

-Toast the walnuts first, and then let them cool. Grind them finely along with ¼ cup of sugar.

-In a small saucepan, cream the butter plus a half cup of sugar. The mixture has to become fluffy and light.

-Add the yolks into the mixture one at a time. Scrape the bowl, especially the sides, and then beat after adding one yolk.

-Fold in the walnuts into the egg and butter mixture. Set aside.

-In a grease-free bowl, whisk the egg whites and slowly add in the last ¼ cup of sugar. You will notice the formation of stiff peaks. Gently fold in this mixture into the butter mixture. Fold in only a little at a time until everything has been fully and evenly mixed.

-Pour the contents into a small Bundt or loaf pan.

-Bake at 350 degrees

Rosemary And Sea Salt Flax Crackers

This makes a lot of crackers that you can enjoy at any time of the day.

Ingredients:

-1 cup milled or ground flax seeds
-2 eggs
-½ cup grated Romano or parmesan cheese
-Kosher or sea salt for sprinkling
-1 teaspoon fresh rosemary, minced

Preparation:

-Preheat the oven to 350 degrees Fahrenheit. Using a nonstick spray, spray 1-2 cookie sheets.

-Add all of the ingredients, except for the salt, in a medium bowl. Stir until everything has been fully combined. Let the mixture sit for about 5 minutes.

-Using nonstick spray, spray a large cutting board or a clean countertop. You should also spray your rolling pin.

-Form the dough into a ball shape and put it on the greased counter.

-Roll it out as thin as you want. The thinnest ones are the best.

-Using a cookie or biscuit cutter, cut a grid of 1 inch squares on the flattened dough.

-Using a pie server or small spatula, transfer the individual squares on the cookie sheets.

-Re-roll the leftover dough and cutting everything until all of the dough is gone.

-Sprinkle the top with salt.-Bake the crackers for 10 minutes; remove from the oven, flip, and then bake 3 minutes.

If you wish your crackers to be very crispy, try turning off the oven and then put the crackers back inside after they have already cooled down a little, but are still warm to touch. You can leave them inside for about an hour and they will simply become dryer and crispier. You can serve this together with a dip or cheese.

Chocolate Mousse Shots

Ingredients:

-1 can coconut milk (full-fat or you can also use coconut cream)
-¼ cup plus 1 tablespoon cocoa or cacao powder
-½ teaspoon pure vanilla extract
-Sweetener (you can use powdered sugar or stevia)

Preparation:

-Open the coconut milk and leave it uncovered in the refrigerator without a cover overnight. This is only applicable if the milk is not as thick as mousse. Remember not to shake the can before you open it.

-Once the milk has thickened, transfer it into a bowl and mix in your vanilla, sweetener, and cocoa. You can do this using a fork or with mixers.

-Pipe the mousse into cute little containers and store them in the fridge to make them even thicker.

Dried Fruit Scones

This recipe makes about 8 delicious and moist scones. The taste is simply marvelous. The outside is crispy and golden in color, while the inside is just plain heavenly.

Ingredients:

2 ¼ cups of brown rice flour
¼ cup of sugar
½ teaspoon of xanthan gum
2 teaspoons of baking powder
¼ teaspoon nutmeg (this is optional)
½ teaspoon of salt
¾ cup of diced dried fruit (depends on your preference)
2 large eggs
½ cup butter, cold
1/3 cup milk, cold
1 teaspoon of vanilla extract (wheat and gluten-free)

Preparation:

- Preheat your oven to 400 degrees Fahrenheit. Grease a baking sheet or line it with parchment paper. You can also use a divided scone pan for this, but you have to grease it properly ahead of time.

- Whisk the flour, xanthan gum, sugar, salt, baking powder, and nutmeg together. Make sure that everything is mixed well.

- Add in the cold butter until the resulting mixture is crumbly in appearance and texture.

- Add in the dry mix into the crumbly mixture.

- In another bowl, add in the vanilla, milk, and the eggs. Mix until frothy.

- Add in the previous mixture into the dry mixture. Stir everything well. Everything should be well-blended. The resulting dough should be very sticky and cohesive.

- Drop the dough onto the scone pan or baking sheet, about 1/3 of a cup at a time. If you choose not to have dried fruit, lessen the amount of dough you add onto the scone pan or baking sheet, just about ¼ of a cup only. Leave the dough to rest for about 15 minutes.

- Add cinnamon sugar or sparkling sugar on the scones before baking them, if you like. Bake them for 15-20 minutes, or until the scones are golden brown in color. Take them out from the oven and let them cool for 5 minutes. You can add butter and jam for a perfect treat!

Petite Raisin-White Chocolate Scones

This is a great twist to the favorite plain scones that people like. These may be small, but you will surely love the taste of these babies! This recipe makes 32 mini raisin-white chocolate scones.

Ingredients:

2 cups wheat-free flour blend
1/3 cup of sugar
1 teaspoon of lemon zest, freshly grated
2 teaspoons of baking powder
½ teaspoon of salt
½ cup of butter, softened
¾ cup raisins, chopped coarsely
¾ cup whipping cream
2 teaspoons of shortening
1 ¼ cups of white baking chocolate chips (preferably gluten-free)

Preparation:

- For the flour blend, combine 2/3 cups of potato starch, 1 teaspoon of xanthan gum, 2 cups of rice flour, and 1/3 cup of tapioca flour. Use only the needed amount of flour blend for this recipe. Stir everything again before using.

- Preheat the oven to 400 degrees Fahrenheit.

- Combine the baking powder, salt, flour blend, sugar, and lemon zest in a large bowl. Add in the butter using a pastry blender or a fork. The resulting mixture will resemble coarse crumbs.

- Add in the whipping cream. Mix everything well until the dough is cohesive. Add in the raisins and ¾ cup of the white baking chocolate chips.

- On a lightly-floured surface, turn the dough. Knead it for about 5-10 times or until the dough is smooth. Divide it into 4 equal parts. Make each part into a log that measures approximately 8-by-1-inch long. Cut each log into 2-inch pieces (4 parts), and then cut each of the squares diagonally in half to make small triangles.

- On an ungreased baking sheet, place the scones at least an inch apart. Bake the scones for about 9-11 minutes until the edges become golden brown. Cool them completely.

- Combine the shortening and the remaining baking chips in a microwaveable bowl. Microwave the mixture on medium, for about 30 seconds. Stir and continue to microwave until the mixture becomes smooth and completely melted. Drizzle the top of the scones with the melted chocolate.

Wheat-Free Recipes For Vegans

A lot of vegans complain that most recipes that are wheat-free only cater to those who are meat eaters. Vegans can still go wheat-free when they want to, without sacrificing quality and taste. Here are some fantastic recipes for vegans (plus the Mushroom Risotto in the previous chapter).

Patatas Bravas (Spicy Potatoes)

Ingredients:

-1 pound russet potatoes, or
-3 medium potatoes
-¼ teaspoon sea salt
-4 teaspoons olive oil, divided
-4-5 garlic cloves
-1 8-ounce can of tomato sauce
-1 ½ teaspoons of sherry vinegar
-Heaping ¼ teaspoon crushed red pepper
-½ teaspoon paprika

Preparation:

-Cut potatoes in half lengthwise, then cut each half again lengthwise.
Slice into segments that are ½ inch in size.

-Over medium heat, heat a large skillet. Add about 2 teaspoons of olive
oil. Once the oil is hot, add the salt and the potatoes. Stir well, and then
spread the potatoes well in a single layer.

-Every 5-10 minutes, give the potatoes a stir and scrape the pan. If you
see that the potatoes are becoming too brown on the outside, you can
lower the heat (medium-low). Cook until the potatoes become crispy
and brown on the outside and soft inside. It takes about 45 minutes to
an hour.

-While the potatoes are cooking, mince the garlic finely. On medium
heat, heat a small saucepan and add 2 teaspoons of olive oil.
-Once hot, add the garlic in the small saucepan and sauté for about a
minute.

-Then, add the vinegar, tomato sauce, and seasonings. Stir well and
then lower the heat. Simmer for about 20 minutes to half an hour in
low heat. Once done, remove the pan from the heat.
-Once the potatoes are cooked, top them with the sauce and serve right
away.

Teriyaki Eggplant Steaks

Ingredients:

-3 small eggplants (globe), with the stems taken out and the eggplants sliced
 crosswise to about ½ inch thick
-¼ cup mirin (or dry white wine or sake)
-¼ cup water
-1/3 cup tamari or soy sauce (gluten-free)
-1 garlic clove (large), minced
-2 small scallions or green onions, minced
-a piece of ginger (about 1 ½ inches long), minced
-Crushed red pepper (a pinch)

Preparation:

-Combine everything in a saucepan, except for the eggplants. When it approaches medium heat, leave the mixture to simmer for about 10 minutes. The sauce will become thicker. Once done, remove from the heat.

-Put the eggplant slices inside a casserole dish. Cover it with the sauce. Leave the eggplants in the marinade for about 1-2 hours, turning them occasionally.

-Using a griddle pan or a large skillet, heat over medium-high heat. Put oil until the pan is filmed lightly. Lay the eggplants on the pan and fry until browned lightly. Flip and then cook for a few more minutes.

-Remove eggplants from heat and set aside. Do the same process with the remaining eggplants all have been fully cooked. Serve.

Mung Bean Stew

Ingredients:

-250 grams mung beans, soaked for a minimum of 6 hours
-1 onion, finely chopped
-½ teaspoon cumin
-½ teaspoon turmeric powder
-1 vegetable stock cube (wheat-free)
-2 carrots, peeled, trimmed, and chopped
-½ butternut squash, deseeded, peeled, and chopped
-1 teaspoon tamari sauce
-2 tablespoons coriander leaves
-1 celery stalk, chopped

Preparation:

-Rinse the mung beans and drain thoroughly.
-Place the mung beans, cumin, turmeric, onion, and vegetable stock inside a saucepan. Bring to a boil in about 750 ml of water. This has to simmer for at least 30 minutes.
-Add the celery, tamari, squash, and carrot, and let the mixture simmer for another 10 minutes.
-You can serve this with brown rice and sprinkle the top with coriander leaves.

Baba Ganoush

This is a very healthy dip for everybody, for any occasion!

Ingredients:

-1 baked eggplant, and then peeled
-½ cup lemon juice
-½ cup tahini paste
-2 garlic cloves minced
-½ teaspoon salt
-1 parsley or mint for garnish
-Olive oil/cayenne pepper on top

Preparation:

-To bake the eggplant, puncture it and roast it using a baking sheet at 400 degrees, for about 40 minutes. The oven should have been preheated to the same temperature.

-Once done, the eggplant should be placed inside a plastic bag as it cools. This helps make the peeling process an easier task.

-In a bowl, add the garlic, tahini paste, lemon juice, and garlic. Place them all in a blender, or if not, use a mortar.

-Spread the baba ganoush in a nice plate and garnish it with mint or parsley.

-This is perfect with olives, or simply as a dip for vegetables.

Feedback From People Who Went On A Wheat Free Diet

There have been a lot of people who have went on a wheat-free diet and have never regretted their decision and never looked back. Many of these people report that they feel healthier and younger than before starting the program. Every day there are more people who are choosing to go wheat-free. They choose to do so, so they can experience how great it is to feel and be healthier.

I challenge you to do a search on the internet and see for yourself how many people have successfully removed wheat from their diets and reaped the benefits. You will be astounded by the number of success stories that people have shared about their experiences as followers of the Wheat Free plan.

Conclusion

The "Lose the Belly Fat Weight Loss Plan" truly shows a lot of promise. Going wheat-free will help many people become and stay healthier. Judging by the enormous amount of testimonials found online, many people every day are choosing to eliminate wheat from their diets. Instead of wheat, they are looking for healthier alternatives. In many countries that use wheat as a staple in their diets it may be a bit more difficult to persuade individuals to give this healthier way of eating a try. However, this has not stopped the "Wheat Free" revolution in the United States and other parts of the world. Just give it a try for 30 days, and you will see how your life will change!

Thank You For Buying This Book

Thank you for purchasing this book. I hope you enjoyed it and now have strategies you can implement to improve your health with your new way of eating Wheat Free.

Would you kindly do me a favor when you have a moment, please review "**WHEAT FREE DIET: Lose the belly fat weight loss plan and wheat free recipe cookbook. Ideal diet for wheat, gluten and food allergy sufferers.**" Then I'll know whether you liked it or not and you will also help others looking for the truth about a Wheat Free program.

You can easily provide a review by going to the following website:

http://joshuacollinshealth.com/wheatfree

Click on the title of the book and then scroll down the page and look on the left side and you will see a button that says "Write a Customer Review". Click on that button and leave your review.

Yours in Health,

Joshua Collins

Recommended Reads

The Paleo Solution: The Original Human Diet by Robb Wolf

The Dash Diet Weight Loss Solution: 2 Weeks to Drop Pounds, Boost Metabolism, and Get Healthy by Marla Heller

The 100: Count ONLY Sugar Calories and Lose Up to 18 Lbs. in 2 Weeks by Jorge Cruise

Other Health Related Books By Joshua Collins

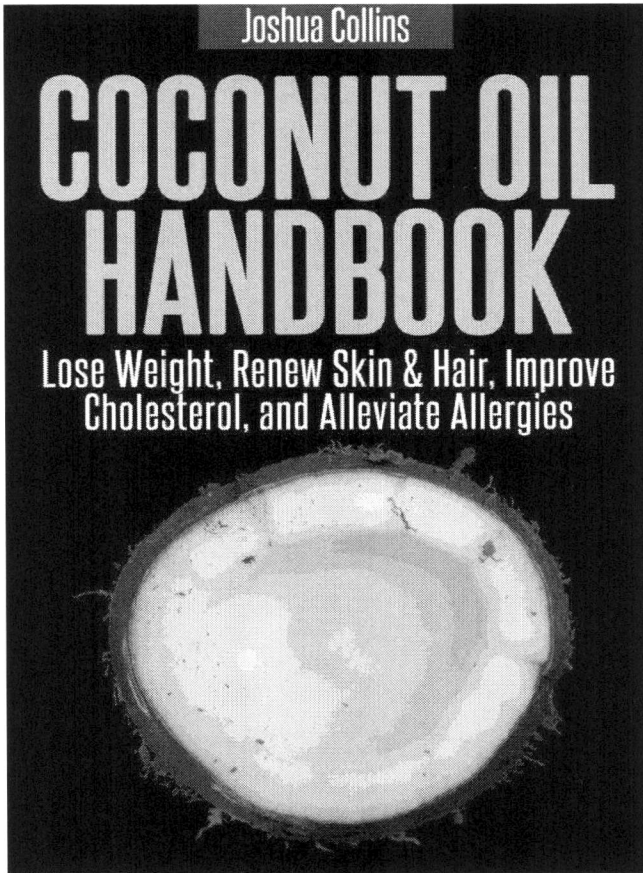

http://joshuacollinshealth.com/coconutoil

Joshua Collins provides everything you ever wanted and needed to know about Coconut Oil. He has also included some awesome recipes and non-medicinal uses for Coconut Oil which can easily be incorporated into your lifestyle. So if you are "sick and tired" of being "sick and tired" this book by Joshua Collins will help you enhance your health.

Medical Disclaimer

This book is intended as a reference guide only and not as a medical manual or medical advice. The sources and information provided in this book are strictly designed to assist you in making informed decisions regarding your overall conditions or problems. Please seek the advice of a qualified medical professional whenever contemplating changes in your medical care or lifestyle. Neither this book, nor the information herein, is intended to replace or substitute any diagnosis, treatment or medication that has been prescribed or recommended by a health care provider, your doctor or a pharmacist. I strongly suggest you check with your medical care provider, pharmacist or doctor and follow their guidelines to create a well-balanced nutritional diet. It is recommended that you consult your health care provider before beginning any new exercise, diet program or regime. Each person has different needs and requirements, based on their overall health situation. Please consult your physician before starting any new health programs.

Printed in Great Britain
by Amazon